EMMANUEL JOSEPH

Symbiotic Prosperity, The Dance of Growth, Wellness, and Time Stewardship

Copyright © 2025 by Emmanuel Joseph

All rights reserved. No part of this publication may be reproduced, stored or transmitted in any form or by any means, electronic, mechanical, photocopying, recording, scanning, or otherwise without written permission from the publisher. It is illegal to copy this book, post it to a website, or distribute it by any other means without permission.

First edition

This book was professionally typeset on Reedsy.
Find out more at reedsy.com

Contents

1	Chapter 1: The Foundations of Symbiotic Prosperity	1
2	Chapter 2: The Essence of Personal Growth	3
3	Chapter 3: Professional Growth: Balancing Ambition and...	5
4	Chapter 4: Emotional Wellness: The Heart of Symbiotic...	7
5	Chapter 5: Time Stewardship: Mastering the Art of Life...	9
6	Chapter 6: The Harmony of Mind, Body, and Spirit	11
7	Chapter 7: The Power of Positive Relationships	13
8	Chapter 8: Financial Wellness: Building a Solid Foundation	15
9	Chapter 9: The Role of Creativity and Innovation	17
10	Chapter 10: The Importance of Rest and Rejuvenation	19
11	Chapter 11: The Power of Gratitude and Positive Thinking	21
12	Chapter 12: The Art of Mindful Living	23
13	Chapter 13: Resilience and Adaptability in the Face of...	25
14	Chapter 14: The Role of Service and Contribution	26
15	Chapter 15: The Journey of Symbiotic Prosperity	27

1

Chapter 1: The Foundations of Symbiotic Prosperity

In the ever-evolving landscape of human progress, one must seek a balanced approach to growth. Growth in isolation is a hollow endeavor, often leading to burnout and disillusionment. Instead, we should envision growth as a multifaceted process—one that encompasses personal development, professional achievements, and emotional well-being. To navigate this intricate dance, we must start by understanding the very essence of symbiotic prosperity, where different facets of our lives thrive in harmony, feeding off each other's successes.

True symbiotic prosperity is not a destination but a continuous journey. It involves the interconnectedness of growth, wellness, and time stewardship. These three pillars form the bedrock upon which we build a life that is not only prosperous in material terms but also fulfilling and meaningful. As we lay these foundations, we must look inward and evaluate our current state of balance. Are we overemphasizing certain areas at the expense of others? Are we mindful of the time we allocate to each aspect of our lives?

Consider the metaphor of a thriving garden. Just as a gardener carefully tends to each plant, ensuring it receives the right amount of sunlight, water, and nutrients, we must cultivate our lives with the same attentiveness. Each facet—personal, professional, and emotional—requires our dedicated effort and conscious nurturing. It is through this symbiotic approach that we can achieve a state of holistic growth, where each area of our life reinforces and enhances the others.

In the chapters that follow, we will delve deeper into the principles of growth, wellness, and time stewardship. We will explore practical strategies, real-life examples, and inspiring stories that demonstrate the power of symbiotic prosperity. By the end of this journey, you will be equipped with the tools and insights needed to cultivate a life that is not only successful but also deeply rewarding.

2

Chapter 2: The Essence of Personal Growth

Personal growth is the catalyst that drives our journey towards symbiotic prosperity. It is the process of becoming more aware, insightful, and purposeful in our actions and decisions. Personal growth requires us to step out of our comfort zones and embrace new challenges and experiences. It demands continuous learning, self-reflection, and the willingness to evolve. In this chapter, we will explore the significance of personal growth and how it influences every aspect of our lives.

At its core, personal growth is about self-discovery and self-improvement. It involves understanding our strengths and weaknesses, setting meaningful goals, and working towards becoming the best version of ourselves. Personal growth is not a linear process; it is filled with ups and downs, successes and setbacks. However, each experience, whether positive or negative, contributes to our development and shapes our character.

One of the key elements of personal growth is cultivating a growth mindset. This mindset, as opposed to a fixed mindset, embraces challenges and views failures as opportunities to learn and grow. It encourages us to persist in the face of obstacles and to see effort as a path to mastery. By adopting a growth mindset, we can unlock our potential and achieve greater levels of success and fulfillment.

In addition to a growth mindset, personal growth also involves setting intentional goals. These goals should be specific, measurable, achievable, relevant, and time-bound (SMART). By setting clear and purposeful goals, we can create a roadmap for our personal growth journey. It is important to regularly review and adjust our goals to ensure they remain aligned with our evolving aspirations and values.

3

Chapter 3: Professional Growth: Balancing Ambition and Contentment

While personal growth is crucial, professional growth is equally important in achieving symbiotic prosperity. Our careers often define a significant part of our identity and can greatly impact our overall sense of well-being. In this chapter, we will delve into the complexities of professional growth and how to strike a balance between ambition and contentment.

Professional growth involves advancing in our careers, acquiring new skills, and achieving our professional goals. It requires a proactive approach, continuous learning, and a willingness to take on new challenges. However, it is essential to recognize that professional growth is not solely about climbing the corporate ladder or accumulating accolades. It is also about finding fulfillment and satisfaction in our work.

One of the key aspects of professional growth is identifying our passions and aligning our careers with them. When we are passionate about our work, we are more likely to be motivated, engaged, and fulfilled. It is important to reflect on our interests, values, and strengths to determine the career path that best aligns with our passions. This alignment can lead to greater job satisfaction and a sense of purpose in our professional lives.

In addition to passion, professional growth also involves developing a strong work-life balance. Ambition and hard work are important, but they should not come at the expense of our well-being and personal lives. It is crucial to set boundaries, manage our time effectively, and prioritize self-care. By achieving a balance between ambition and contentment, we can thrive in our careers while maintaining a healthy and fulfilling personal life.

4

Chapter 4: Emotional Wellness: The Heart of Symbiotic Prosperity

Emotional wellness is a fundamental component of symbiotic prosperity. It encompasses our ability to manage our emotions, build healthy relationships, and cope with life's challenges. Emotional wellness is not just the absence of mental health issues; it is the presence of positive emotions, resilience, and a sense of well-being. In this chapter, we will explore the importance of emotional wellness and how to cultivate it in our lives.

Emotional wellness begins with self-awareness. It involves recognizing and understanding our emotions, as well as the impact they have on our thoughts and behaviors. By developing emotional intelligence, we can better manage our emotions and respond to situations in a constructive manner. This self-awareness also enables us to identify and address any emotional issues that may be affecting our well-being.

Building healthy relationships is another crucial aspect of emotional wellness. Strong, supportive relationships provide us with a sense of belonging and security. They offer us a safe space to share our feelings, seek advice, and receive support. It is important to nurture our relationships by practicing effective communication, empathy, and mutual respect. By fostering meaningful connections, we can enhance our emotional well-being and create a support system that helps us navigate life's challenges.

Resilience is a key component of emotional wellness. It is the ability to bounce back from setbacks and adapt to adversity. Resilience can be cultivated through various practices, such as mindfulness, positive thinking, and self-care. By building resilience, we can better cope with stress and maintain our emotional well-being, even in difficult times.

5

Chapter 5: Time Stewardship: Mastering the Art of Life Balance

Time stewardship is the practice of managing our time effectively and intentionally. It is about making conscious choices about how we spend our time to ensure that it aligns with our values, goals, and priorities. Time stewardship is not just about being efficient; it is about being purposeful and deliberate in how we allocate our time. In this chapter, we will explore the principles of time stewardship and how to master the art of life balance.

The first step in time stewardship is understanding where our time goes. This involves tracking our daily activities and identifying any patterns or time-wasting habits. By gaining a clear picture of how we spend our time, we can make informed decisions about where to make adjustments. It is important to regularly review and reflect on our time usage to ensure it remains aligned with our priorities.

Setting clear and realistic goals is another essential aspect of time stewardship. These goals should be aligned with our values and long-term aspirations. By setting priorities and focusing on what truly matters, we can avoid getting caught up in unimportant tasks or distractions. It is also important to break our goals into manageable steps and create a schedule or plan to achieve them. This structured approach helps us stay organized and make steady progress towards our goals.

Time stewardship also involves learning to say no. It is easy to become overwhelmed by taking on too many commitments or trying to please everyone. It is important to recognize our limits and prioritize our own well-being. By setting boundaries and being selective about how we spend our time, we can reduce stress and create more space for activities that bring us joy and fulfillment.

6

Chapter 6: The Harmony of Mind, Body, and Spirit

Achieving true symbiotic prosperity requires us to nurture not just our minds, but also our bodies and spirits. This holistic approach to wellness ensures that all aspects of our being are in harmony, creating a balanced and fulfilling life. In this chapter, we will delve into the interconnectedness of mind, body, and spirit and how to cultivate their well-being.

The mind is the epicenter of our thoughts, emotions, and perceptions. It is essential to engage in activities that stimulate our intellect and enhance our cognitive abilities. Reading, learning new skills, and engaging in creative pursuits can keep our minds sharp and agile. Additionally, practicing mindfulness and meditation can help us manage stress and maintain mental clarity.

Our bodies are the vessels that carry us through life. Physical wellness involves maintaining a healthy lifestyle through regular exercise, balanced nutrition, and adequate rest. Exercise not only strengthens our bodies but also releases endorphins that boost our mood and energy levels. A nutritious diet provides the essential nutrients our bodies need to function optimally. Adequate rest allows our bodies to recover and rejuvenate, ensuring we have the energy to pursue our goals.

Spiritual wellness encompasses our sense of purpose, values, and connection to something greater than ourselves. It involves exploring our beliefs, seeking meaning in life, and finding inner peace. This can be achieved through practices such as meditation, prayer, or spending time in nature. Cultivating spiritual wellness helps us stay grounded and centered, allowing us to navigate life's challenges with grace and resilience.

7

Chapter 7: The Power of Positive Relationships

Relationships are the threads that weave the fabric of our lives. Positive relationships enhance our emotional well-being, provide support during difficult times, and enrich our experiences. In this chapter, we will explore the importance of nurturing healthy relationships and how to build and maintain them.

Strong relationships are built on trust, communication, and mutual respect. It is important to be open and honest with our loved ones, expressing our thoughts and feelings in a constructive manner. Active listening is a crucial skill that allows us to truly understand and empathize with others. By being present and attentive, we can build deeper connections and foster a sense of belonging.

In addition to communication, it is important to practice empathy and compassion in our relationships. Understanding and valuing the perspectives and experiences of others can strengthen our bonds and create a supportive and loving environment. Small acts of kindness and gratitude can go a long way in nurturing positive relationships.

It is also important to set healthy boundaries in our relationships. Boundaries help us protect our well-being and maintain a sense of autonomy. By clearly communicating our needs and limits, we can prevent misunderstandings and conflicts. Healthy boundaries allow us to engage in relationships that are respectful, supportive, and fulfilling.

8

Chapter 8: Financial Wellness: Building a Solid Foundation

Financial wellness is a critical component of symbiotic prosperity. It involves managing our finances in a way that supports our goals and values while providing security and peace of mind. In this chapter, we will explore the principles of financial wellness and how to build a solid financial foundation.

The first step in achieving financial wellness is creating a budget. A budget helps us track our income and expenses, ensuring that we live within our means. By setting financial goals and prioritizing our spending, we can make informed decisions about how to allocate our resources. It is important to regularly review and adjust our budget to reflect changes in our financial situation and goals.

Saving and investing are also key aspects of financial wellness. Saving provides a safety net for unexpected expenses and helps us achieve our long-term financial goals. Investing allows our money to grow over time, building wealth and financial security. It is important to educate ourselves about different investment options and seek professional advice if needed.

Managing debt is another important aspect of financial wellness. While some debt, such as a mortgage or student loans, can be beneficial, excessive debt can be a burden. It is important to understand the terms of our debt and develop a plan to pay it off. By managing debt responsibly, we can reduce financial stress and improve our overall well-being.

9

Chapter 9: The Role of Creativity and Innovation

Creativity and innovation are the driving forces behind progress and personal fulfillment. They allow us to think outside the box, solve problems, and bring new ideas to life. In this chapter, we will explore the importance of nurturing creativity and innovation in our lives and how they contribute to symbiotic prosperity.

Creativity is not limited to the arts; it can be applied to any area of life, from problem-solving in the workplace to finding new ways to connect with loved ones. It involves thinking differently, taking risks, and embracing the unknown. Cultivating creativity requires an open mind, curiosity, and a willingness to experiment and make mistakes.

Innovation, on the other hand, is the process of turning creative ideas into practical solutions. It involves taking a fresh approach to existing challenges and developing new ways of doing things. Innovation requires critical thinking, collaboration, and a proactive attitude. By fostering an environment that encourages creativity and innovation, we can drive personal and professional growth.

One way to nurture creativity and innovation is to create a space for exploration and play. This can be as simple as setting aside time for brainstorming sessions, engaging in creative hobbies, or exposing ourselves to new experiences and perspectives. Additionally, seeking feedback and collaborating with others can provide valuable insights and inspire new ideas.

10

Chapter 10: The Importance of Rest and Rejuvenation

In our fast-paced world, it is easy to overlook the importance of rest and rejuvenation. However, taking time to recharge is essential for maintaining our well-being and sustaining our productivity. In this chapter, we will explore the significance of rest and how to incorporate it into our lives.

Rest is not just about sleep; it encompasses any activity that allows us to relax and recharge. This can include physical rest, such as taking breaks from work or engaging in gentle activities, as well as mental rest, such as practicing mindfulness or spending time in nature. Rest allows our bodies and minds to recover from the demands of daily life, reducing stress and preventing burnout.

Rejuvenation, on the other hand, involves engaging in activities that bring us joy and fulfillment. This can include hobbies, creative pursuits, or spending time with loved ones. Rejuvenation helps us reconnect with our passions and interests, providing a sense of purpose and satisfaction. By prioritizing rest and rejuvenation, we can maintain our energy levels and enhance our overall well-being.

Incorporating rest and rejuvenation into our lives requires a deliberate and mindful approach. It is important to set boundaries and create a balance between work and leisure. This can involve setting aside dedicated time for rest, creating a restful environment, and being mindful of our energy levels and needs. By making rest and rejuvenation a priority, we can sustain our well-being and thrive in all areas of our lives.

11

Chapter 11: The Power of Gratitude and Positive Thinking

Gratitude and positive thinking are powerful tools for enhancing our well-being and achieving symbiotic prosperity. They help us shift our focus from what is lacking to what is abundant in our lives, fostering a sense of contentment and fulfillment. In this chapter, we will explore the benefits of gratitude and positive thinking and how to cultivate them.

Gratitude involves recognizing and appreciating the positive aspects of our lives. It can be as simple as acknowledging the small joys and blessings we encounter each day. Practicing gratitude helps us develop a more positive outlook, reducing stress and increasing our overall sense of well-being. It can also strengthen our relationships by fostering a sense of appreciation and connection.

Positive thinking, on the other hand, involves focusing on the good and finding solutions rather than dwelling on problems. It is not about ignoring challenges, but rather approaching them with a constructive and optimistic mindset. Positive thinking can boost our resilience, improve our mood, and enhance our overall well-being.

To cultivate gratitude and positive thinking, it is helpful to develop daily habits and practices. This can include keeping a gratitude journal, expressing appreciation to others, and practicing mindfulness and positive affirmations. By making gratitude and positive thinking a regular part of our lives, we can enhance our well-being and create a more fulfilling and joyful life.

12

Chapter 12: The Art of Mindful Living

Mindful living involves being fully present and engaged in each moment, cultivating a deep sense of awareness and appreciation for life. It allows us to connect with ourselves and the world around us, enhancing our overall well-being and sense of fulfillment. In this chapter, we will explore the principles of mindful living and how to incorporate them into our daily lives.

Mindfulness involves paying attention to our thoughts, emotions, and physical sensations without judgment. It helps us become more aware of our experiences and reactions, allowing us to respond rather than react to situations. Mindfulness can be practiced through various techniques, such as meditation, deep breathing, and mindful movement.

Mindful living extends beyond formal mindfulness practices; it involves bringing a sense of presence and intention to all aspects of our lives. This can include being fully present in our interactions with others, savoring the simple pleasures of life, and being mindful of our actions and choices. By practicing mindful living, we can cultivate a deeper sense of connection, gratitude, and fulfillment.

Incorporating mindful living into our daily lives requires a deliberate and intentional approach. It is important to create opportunities for mindfulness, such as setting aside time for meditation, practicing mindful eating, and engaging in activities that promote mindfulness. By making mindful living a priority, we can enhance our well-being and create a more balanced and fulfilling life.

13

Chapter 13: Resilience and Adaptability in the Face of Change

Change is an inevitable part of life, and our ability to adapt and thrive in the face of change is crucial for symbiotic prosperity. Resilience and adaptability enable us to navigate life's challenges and uncertainties with grace and confidence. In this chapter, we will explore the importance of resilience and adaptability and how to cultivate them.

Resilience is the ability to bounce back from setbacks and maintain a positive outlook despite difficulties. It involves developing coping mechanisms, such as problem-solving skills, emotional regulation, and a strong support network. By building resilience, we can better manage stress, overcome obstacles, and emerge stronger from adversity.

Adaptability, on the other hand, is the ability to adjust to new situations and embrace change. It requires a flexible mindset, open-mindedness, and a willingness to learn and grow. Adaptability allows us to seize new opportunities and thrive in an ever-changing world. By cultivating adaptability, we can remain agile and resilient in the face of change.

14

Chapter 14: The Role of Service and Contribution

Service and contribution are powerful components of symbiotic prosperity. They allow us to connect with others, make a positive impact, and find deeper meaning in our lives. In this chapter, we will explore the significance of service and contribution and how they enhance our well-being and sense of fulfillment.

Service involves giving our time, energy, and resources to help others and make a difference in our communities. It can take many forms, from volunteering and charitable work to acts of kindness and mentorship. Service allows us to develop empathy, compassion, and a sense of purpose. By serving others, we can create a positive ripple effect that benefits both ourselves and those around us.

Contribution, on the other hand, involves using our skills, talents, and passions to create value and make a meaningful impact. It can involve pursuing a career that aligns with our values, sharing our knowledge and expertise, or supporting causes we care about. Contribution allows us to feel a sense of accomplishment and fulfillment, knowing that we are making a difference in the world.

15

Chapter 15: The Journey of Symbiotic Prosperity

The journey of symbiotic prosperity is an ongoing process of growth, wellness, and time stewardship. It involves continuously seeking balance, embracing new challenges, and nurturing all aspects of our lives. In this final chapter, we will reflect on the principles and practices we have explored and how to integrate them into our daily lives.

Achieving symbiotic prosperity requires a holistic and intentional approach. It involves being mindful of our goals, values, and priorities and making conscious choices that align with them. It requires a commitment to personal and professional growth, emotional wellness, time stewardship, and service to others. By integrating these principles into our lives, we can create a balanced, fulfilling, and meaningful existence.

The journey of symbiotic prosperity is not about perfection; it is about progress and continuous improvement. It involves celebrating our successes, learning from our setbacks, and remaining open to new possibilities. It is about living a life that is true to ourselves and aligned with our deepest values and aspirations.

Book Description: Symbiotic Prosperity: The Dance of Growth, Wellness, and Time Stewardship

In "Symbiotic Prosperity: The Dance of Growth, Wellness, and Time

Stewardship," you will embark on a transformative journey towards achieving a balanced and fulfilling life. This book explores the interconnectedness of personal growth, professional development, emotional wellness, and time stewardship, providing practical strategies and insights to help you thrive in all areas of your life.

Through thoughtful reflections, real-life examples, and inspiring stories, you will learn how to cultivate a growth mindset, develop meaningful relationships, manage your finances, nurture your creativity, and practice mindful living. The principles and practices outlined in this book will empower you to navigate life's challenges with resilience and adaptability, finding deeper meaning and fulfillment along the way.

"Symbiotic Prosperity" is a guide to living a life that is not only successful but also deeply rewarding. Whether you are seeking to enhance your personal growth, achieve professional success, or find a sense of balance and well-being, this book offers the tools and insights you need to create a harmonious and prosperous life.

www.ingramcontent.com/pod-product-compliance
Lightning Source LLC
LaVergne TN
LVHW020740090526
838202LV00057BA/6152